ALSO BY WALTER MOSLEY

life out

WHICH INCLUDES A PROPOSAL FOR THE NON-VIOLENT

WALTER MOSLEY

•

of context

Takeover of the House of Representatives

Nation Books / New York

LIFE OUT OF CONTEXT
*Which Includes a Proposal for the Non-violent Takeover
of the House of Representatives*

Published by
Nation Books
An Imprint of Avalon Publishing Group
245 West 17th St., 11th Floor
New York, NY 10011

Copyright © 2006 by Walter Mosley

First printing January 2006

Nation Books is a co-publishing venture of the Nation Institute and
Avalon Publishing Group Incorporated.

Library of Congress Cataloging-in-Publication Data is available.

ISBN: 1-56025-846-2
ISBN 13: 978-1-56025-846-9

9 8 7 6 5 4 3 2

BOOK DESIGN BY PAULINE NEUWIRTH

Printed in the United States of America
Distributed by Publishers Group West

For Donna Masini

I would like to thank Kimiko Hahn for her help
with the quote from Walt Whitman, which is from the
150th anniversary edition of the first printing of *Leaves of Grass*.

The sum of all known value and respect I add up in you
    whoever you are;
The president is up there in the White House for you . . . not you
    here for him,
The secretaries act in their bureaus for you . . . not you
    here for them,
The Congress convenes every December for you,
Laws, courts, the forming of states, the charter of cities,
    the going and coming of commerce and mails are all
    for you.

WALT WHITMAN
Leaves of Grass

0.

THIS MONOGRAPH WAS written over a very short period of time. It was a feverish episode in which I felt it necessary to uncover and articulate methods we could employ to make the world safer for the millions who are needlessly suffering. It seems to me that each and every one of us needs to consider our potential to make a better world because the ones who lead us are themselves in dire need of direction.

What follows, as you shall see, is a political work anchored in some very personal and even pedestrian experiences.

All political activity is based upon prosaic human experience. We get involved in politics to better our situation and possibly to help others. Accepting this notion as a given, I tried to connect my personal struggles with how I perceive political realities in the United States and beyond.

Another important aspect of this essay is that I am not an expert in domestic and foreign affairs. It is essential, I believe, that everyday citizens discuss our political reality without the input and guidance of so-called experts. This is because experts in our current political environment are just as likely to mislead as they are to lead; they misinform as often as they enlighten.

I use as my example Colin Powell standing before the world pointing at little yellow dots in the desert in Iraq. Those yellow dots, we were told by the emperor of experts, were proof positive that there were weapons of mass destruction stored within our enemy's borders; weapons that could very likely be used against Americans on American soil.

Powell was the ultimate expert. Everyday citizens—with no infrared spycam satellites at our disposal, with no battery of PhDs to advise us—could not argue with the secretary of state. His working example that we were in imminent danger of a devastating attack from Iraq could not be ignored.

But still we hesitated. We cried out that even if there

had to be a limited war, we still didn't want innocents to die; after all, our enemies were the dictatorial leaders of that nation and not its citizens. In response, our master expert told us that our bombs were too smart to do something like murder an innocent man or child. Our bombs were experts at sparing the innocent.

While we ordinary folks wondered how smart you would have to be to translate a yellow dot into a world-challenging threat, we missed the salient fact—Colin Powell was lying to us. He must have known that those dots might have been something other than WMDs: maybe giant aerosol cans or soft-serve ice cream containers. They could have been so many kegs of Iraqi beer.

The secretary of state and his army of experts are too smart to have made that big of a gaffe. No. These men and women are experts in the modern sense. They interpret the data to benefit the people to whom they are beholden.

Modern-day experts are not interested in the truth. Their only goal is to prove a point of view.

If this argument is true, then we cannot rely on political and military experts when trying to understand and improve upon our world. These men and women will consciously leave out the truth in order to gain our support.

In the case of Iraq, that support has led to the deaths of thousands, all of whom, in relation to us, were innocent.

●

So I took it upon myself to thrash around, trying to come up with a method that might help us to make decisions separate from the so-called experts and their masters. What I have come up with is a way of thinking connected to a few ideas that might have a deep impact upon our political reality.

I make many suggestions in the pages that follow, but I believe that if there is any value in this piece, it comes from a way of thinking and not necessarily the thoughts themselves.

But before you get there, you have to come with me to a few artistic gatherings which were the germs in my genesis of thought.

1.

THE OTHER NIGHT, I attended a lecture given by one of America's premier Public Intellectuals. It was an interesting talk with lots of visual aids and some brilliant examples of art. I went because attending these public presentations has become a regular event for me and a good friend. It's almost a custom with us. Sometimes friendship needs custom to hold it together. We attend the talk, almost always have dinner afterwards, and discuss ideas—maybe having to do with the presentation, maybe not.

This particular evening we went on a tangent at dinner. I was saying that a writer we had run into at the event had a cultural, intellectual, artistic, and professional context in which he saw himself. Because of this self-perception, his chosen friends were all of a certain success level and ilk and they all supported each other in, what seemed to me, a very calculated way. He, and his friends, would be happy to talk about the lineage and history of their styles of writing and where they had broadened and deepened the genre.

My friend didn't agree. She said that the writer in question merely had friends who thought like he did, people he liked.

I said that most writers, and other artists for that matter, portrayed themselves in a broader (or maybe narrower) context. I used as an example a writer we both knew who compared himself with the masters of ancient Greek tragedy. If you threw doubt on his work, he would argue that you are also bringing into question the great historical masters of the art.

It's a convenient trick. Sophocles and his buddies are all gone. And it is true that they created unrivaled masterpieces. The question is, of course, does this contemporary writer, who compares himself with these long-dead playwrights, have some reasonable argument that can make us equate his prose with their work?

Many critics think so. They laud the contemporary writer and his writing. He, in turn, speaks fondly of the old masters. It all comes out rather well. There are no loose ends—at least not for the writers who have found, or staked out, their context.

I DIDN'T REALLY care about the circumstances that these artists make use of to promote and justify their work. I was interested in the reasoning behind their fabricated affiliations, which I readily admit I only supposed.

One value in belonging to a group is professional. You have friends who hire you, write you letters of recommendation, excuse your shortcomings, and profess love for the work you commit. These artists affiliate themselves with institutions whose boards create endowments which help to foster the work of these writers. These professional friends influence awards, stipends, and subtler decisions that bring, at least for a moment, these works and their creators into the public eye.

I realize that this is a cynical opinion, but I can't help that. My experience tells me that even the arts are tainted by greed, need, and the jealous protection of intellectual preserves.

Another use of an artistic context was more interesting to me that particular evening. I saw that the speaker, that venerable Public Intellectual, wasn't the only one who benefited from the context in which he saw himself and in which he was seen: his audience also seemed to profit.

The people in attendance were willing to believe in him and what he professed. His complex notions and moral convictions were given great weight. People around him strove to understand his meaning. And in this striving they were bound to gain something, even if the lecture ultimately meant nothing; this because he was seen in a context with, and compared himself to, certain other writers and artists.

The same was true for the writer we ran into and also the writer who lives in the ether of the ancient Greeks. All of them benefit from an intellectual and artistic structure that lends an authority and a breadth to their work that few lone artists could accomplish. Their readers and students also gain because of a group of dynamic ideas that blossom *within a context* of art and artists.

I mean, didn't my friend and I use the context of that public talk to give meaning and a certain weight to our relationship? Surely. There was, I concluded, nothing wrong with bolstering a solitary agenda of creativity with a larger system of thinkers and thought—even if the claims of the system in question are dubious.

LATER ON THAT evening, when I was walking home, I realized that I was oppressed by this notion of a literary context. I felt left out, hapless because I had no school of thought, ancient masters, or even many writer friends who I could consider to be a context for the work I do. I wasn't part of a movement. And when I thought about my own work—which ranges from crime stories to short stories to so-called literary fiction to science fiction to works like the one you're reading here—I can hardly find a context between one book and the next.

The people I had seen and talked about that night had no loose ends, where the fabric of my career was like a hopelessly knotted wad of dirty string. As the evening went on, I felt more and more miserable. It was that moment of self-indulgence where someone with absolutely nothing to complain about stacks his little bundle of success next to someone else's and asks, "Why don't I have the things that he has?"

I spent much of the next few hours in that self-indulgent mood. I'm not proud of it, but I believe that it's necessary to bare my feelings so that I can come to a greater realization about my own failings and therefore my chances for liberation.

The night became early morning. I slept, but even my dreams were unsettled, unanchored. At dawn, however, I woke up without a care. Somewhere in the night I decided, not consciously, to accept the disarray of my work, such as it is. I don't know why I read books, why I write them or love having them in my home. I rarely know what story it is that I'm going to tell next. These are the facts of my professional life. There is for me a deep well of pre-literature that I dredge up every morning. I can't predict what I will find in my bucket. I can't throw back what I discover or go looking for something else, something more in line with writers I love or want to be friends with. I am stuck with what I have. Each morning I lumber naked to my computer, set on a squat table, and begin writing what I can.

I had finished with the malady of envy and hunger for others' success.

The contexts of other writers' lives are closed to me. I don't associate with them. I don't do work that would get me access to their clubs. There's nothing else to say about it.

My life would go on the way it had, filled with contradictions and seemingly nonsensical juxtapositions—and that was, finally, just fine by me.

2.

THE NEXT DAY, I got a call from Clyde Taylor, a friend and professor of American Studies at NYU. He told me that our good friend Manthia Diawara had come back from Ghana, where he'd been teaching for the past year. Manthia was going to show his new documentary film, *Conakry Kas*, at the Museum of Modern Art later that evening.

In the film, Dr. Diawara took on an extraordinarily complex and convoluted subject: the multifaceted character of Africa and how the quixotic temperaments of that continent hobble attempts to unite peoples who have been saddled with contradictory self-images by religious, political, and imperialist colonization. The failure at unification, Diawara's film in part postulates, is further exacerbated by plagues and international racism which have not been at all moderated by the ever-growing spectre of globalization.

The film concentrated on Guinea and in particular the crazy-quilt city of Conakry. In the narrative, Dr. Diawara covered everything from foreign and folk music to the nationalism-turned-socialism-turned-dictatorship of the powerful and charismatic leader Sekou Toure. He showed us rap singers in the streets improvising protest songs, and the victims and proponents of Toure. There were represented African voices of all ages and social castes, genders, and tribal groupings. They discussed everything from world-wide economics to the inaccuracy of the term *tribalism*.

I was floored by the breadth of the piece and more than a little daunted by the complexity of the issues and dangers faced on a daily basis by tens of millions of people who, on the one hand, have more than enough power, intelligence, and natural resources to conquer their problems but, on the other hand, have no overriding concept that will allow them to come together and throw off the centuries of maddening Western and Middle Eastern domination.

Africa, Diawara's film suggested, was a continent in search of a context.

AFTER THE FILM, seven of us went to dinner. We were three Africans, an India Indian, and three American Blacks.

The thing I remember most about the evening is that we laughed a lot. Someone said that they had it on good authority that the National Republican Party was thinking seriously of running Condoleezza Rice for president. We talked about Iraq and the problems the people of color in the United States had getting together to address their social, political, and economic woes. But no matter what we talked about, we found humor in it all. We were all the descendants of oppressed peoples and knew instinctually that when you forget how to laugh you have been defeated. I laughed hard and almost forgot about the heartbreaking truths of Dr. Diawara's documentary.

AT THE END of the evening, almost as an afterthought, Manthia turned to me and asked, "Are you coming to the talk between Harry Belafonte and Hugh Masekela tomorrow at NYU?"

I said that would be nice.

Manthia then added, "Okay. We'll put your name at the door and, as long as you're coming, why don't you introduce them?"

This is the way Clyde, Manthia, and I interact. We take rather large events and make them seem small and matter-of-fact.

"Sure," I said.

I WALKED HOME again. This time I was wondering what I would say about the two great intellectuals and performers who have so informed the African Diaspora of the latter half of the twentieth century and helped so many to understand the heartbreak of those scattered and sundered peoples.

I thought about it for a while—until I realized that my function was a simple one. I'd say: "Ladies and gentlemen, I present to you two men that I love and admire. Please welcome . . ." and that would be it.

And so when I got home and went to bed, I fully expected to fall asleep. After all, Harry and Hugh were examples of the giant interlacing contexts of jazz and political activism, and they were the nexuses for many of the major players in those areas for the past fifty years and more. It was their show and they knew how to run it. I didn't have a thing to worry about.

I would have fallen asleep had I not been reminded of the word *context*.

Harry Belafonte, I knew from Manthia's film, had been going to Guinea since Sekou Toure took power from the French. He had seen the bright hope and senseless devastation of this brilliant African prince. Hugh Masekela had played music in the streets of Conakry in the seventies. They had both witnessed the great Guinean hope falter and trip on the streets of Africa's expectations.

Context. The Africans I'd seen in Professor Diawara's film were elements in many different and conflicting contexts. Young people at risk and impoverished in a world that knows nothing about them and that cares even less. The descendants of post-colonials, they are tribal and national, modern and traditional, monogamous at heart but polygamous by necessity, waiting for the world to see their worth and just about out of time. Brilliant, beautiful, and tragic, they are my brothers and sisters who cannot move in harmony because their world has been made dissonant by so many foreign and internal pressures.

HIV colors their freedom. Corruption leads them, and religion plucks at their heartstrings. Foreigners, who have no knowledge of their complex cultures, dismiss them for being tribal. Hope is their greatest enemy because to hope is to allow the possibility of failure into their hearts.

The contexts of the writers I had seen and thought about the day before were simple things, well focused on what success looked like. "I am like him," the writer says of himself in a practice run for the reading later on. "My work builds upon his and you should see me like that and think of me in those terms."

The writer can be single-minded in her quest for identity. She accepts some, rejects others, and is resolute in her rightness and her right to belong.

Little more than twenty-four hours have passed, and now I see how silly I'd been to worry about my *place* in the literary landscape. Who I am in that world is meaningless as long as hope and happiness, security and health are denied these millions of young Africans who have been shunted down avenues without exits, into auditoriums where all that is professed is untrue.

What I should be looking for is something that will help me to articulate a context for those millions in the motherland and the millions more that have been scattered and dispossessed.

Last night I was right, in my sleeplessness, to search for a context—it was just that I was thinking too small: I was worried about personal aggrandizement and gain, not about the greater, much more complex good.

I realized, after reflecting on Manthia's film, that I am living in a time that has no driving social framework for a greater good. There are many, many disparate notions about how to make a better world, but these are just so many voices singing a thousand songs in different keys, registers, and styles—a choir of Bedlam.

Many of us seek to make our own lives better; we succeed often enough when we have America behind us. But even if we make a good living and buy a big house, how can our lives be seen as good when so many are starving and suffering, ailing and disinherited?

The digital display said 2:39 A.M. and I was still awake. I turned on the Cartoon Channel to watch the PG-rated animations of Adult Swim. Their cynicism about human nature, which usually made me laugh, gave me the shudders and I had to turn it off.

3.

BY THE NEXT day I was exhausted. I was getting less than four hours of sleep a night and that's not enough for me. I was thinking about my aging mother and the sky-high rents of Manhattan, Conakry and the Ancient Greeks. And there was, of course, the issue of having to introduce two of the premier performers of the second half of the twentieth century.

I also had my daily regimen of three hours of writing to accomplish.

If I don't write, I feel that I'm not participating in my own, internal, life. Somewhere along the way I did learn that there is a personal context for me, and that background is writing. I wake up in the morning, in this skin filled with desires that have no immediate language. Finding that language is my job if not my destiny, and failing to write is as serious a crime as a sentry going to sleep at his post during wartime.

"Who are you, soldier?" the commanding officer demands of the drowsy sentry.

He gives a rank and a name expecting, and accepting, some sort of discipline.

Who am I? I am the man who writes these words.

I GOT THREE bios through E-mail. One for Mr. Belafonte, one for Hugh Masekela, and another for the poet and all-around artist Quincy Troupe (Manthia forgot to mention that Quincy was moderating the dialogue between the musicians.[1])

I received over twenty pages of single-spaced, tiny-font printing. To read those pages out loud would have taken me more than forty minutes, and I knew that no one was coming to hear me talk. I tried to make bullet points out of the fabulous careers of the three men. Number-one hit songs and awards for performance, political activism

---

[1] I call them musicians, but the word has much more meaning than it does in our shallow culture. In the old world, musicians stood at the gateway to the gods. This is what I mean by the word here.

and close calls with the Man. There was too much to say and there was no heart in the details. Finally I decided upon the following stanzas:

... my province is the world of language, prose in particular. My involvement with the written word makes me aware of the uses of communication. Most often the language we use speaks to us, teaches us, enlightens us, tugs at our emotions. This is true for all kinds of communication, from sign language to classical piano recitals. But every once in a while there comes a communicator who goes beyond the *me speaking to you* into a realm where the music seems to know who you are. It mirrors you and allows you to see into your own heart. This for me is the musical genius and commitment of Hugh Masekela ...

... when preparing to introduce Mr. Belafonte, I came across two astonishing facts. The first was that Harry could be president if he wanted. He was born in the United States, something I never knew. This gives me hope somehow. If Harry could be president then maybe we could be saved from ourselves. The second thing I found was that the name

Belafonte is in the spellchecker of my computer's dictionary. Mosley's not there. You have to be either famous or vanilla plain (i.e., John Smith) to be in Microsoft's spellchecker.[2]

Harry's music differs slightly, I feel, from his friend's. Harry's music is buried deep in our unconscious. His mellifluous tones and cool phrasings touch within us some deep wish-fulfillment that we dare not allow to completely emerge. That's because Mr. Belafonte is the best of us and his rhythms cannot be denied, though even in our greatest moments we may not find ourselves to be equal to his courage . . .

. . . Quincy Troupe is a poet. From the basketball court to the metered line to the protest line, his rhymes and reasons break past any false affectations of effete art. Quincy once said to a group of eager would-be poets, "If you want to be a poet you have know what a poem is. . . . Some of you might write, I hate Bush. That might be true—but it's not poetry." He once told an assembly that many times the genius of art is right in our

---

[2] A few nights after I delivered this introduction, I was in Los Angeles having dinner with Hugh and his family. His wife, Elinam, told me that her spellchecker failed to find Belafonte in its lists.

face but we still miss it. He used the example of Jimi Hendrix playing his interpretation of *The Star-Spangled Banner* at Woodstock.

"If I asked you what kind of musician Hendrix was," Quincy said, "you would call him a rock musician. But on that day he transcended rock. He was playing new music like John Cage with no history or training. He did that on the stage and no one even commented on it."

Quincy is also a publisher, an educator, a radical mind, and a saint.

I include these few words in this monograph because composing them was part of the process of my thinking about context. The men coming together on that NYU dais represented a dimension of influence in my intellectual, artistic, and political life that made me want to understand what framework I might build to contain the answer to why we, human beings in the modern world, are so disconnected; why we are so powerful when it comes to destruction and yet so weak and ineffectual when children suffer and die.

I GOT TO the hall early. The woman who said that she'd meet me at the door never came. So I sat there waiting for someone to guide me in.

I felt listless for the most part and a little nervous that one of the officials at the student center might come up and challenge my right to be there. I worried also that my remarks had given short shrift to the long careers of the three men I was introducing.

The fact of my fears made me wonder about them. Why wouldn't the speakers like what I had to say if those words came from my heart? And what reason would the security guards have to pick me out of the dozens of people wandering in and out of the entranceway of the student center?

I remembered being a young adolescent, thirteen years old or so. My mother (who is Jewish by descent) had a cousin named Lily who lived a couple of miles north and west of our house. I loved Lily. She stuffed me full of knishes and candies, garlic baked chicken and homemade cookies. She knew all of the stories of my mother's side of the family, and the way she told them was humorous and warmhearted. Everyone had a flaw in their character but somehow, the way Lily talked about them, their flaws just made them more lovable.

When I was much younger, my favorite thing to do was to go to Lily's house with my mother (and sometimes my father) and play in her backyard under the tremendous avocado tree or next to her ornamental Japanese pool with its giant orange and yellow and black carp.

Now that I was old enough, I would go up to Lily's on

my own once every couple of months or so. I'd walk or ride my bicycle. When you're a child, time has no limit, it seems. I could spend all Saturday migrating to and from Lily's house.

But there was a catch.

In traveling the distance between my house and Lily's, I crossed an invisible border between where Black people were allowed to be and where they shouldn't be. There was no place where Black people *should* be—only the distance between what was allowable and forbidden.

When I crossed Olympic Boulevard, I entered the forbidden zone. More often than not, the police would stop me, question me, and then, in classic police fashion, question my answers.

"What are you doing in this neighborhood?"

"Goin' to visit my cousin."

"Where does this cousin live?"

"On Orlando."

"What's his name?"

"It's a woman. Her name is Lillian Keller."

"How long has she lived there?"

"I don't know. A long time."

The policemen (who were always white) then changed their tactic. A crime had been committed. A kid had been witnessed leaving the scene. They were suspicious of me. I remember once I was riding my J. C. Higgins three-speed, wearing shorts and a T-shirt. I was not what you'd call a great physical specimen. I was five-four or so with no muscle tone whatsoever. The police, after asking the first volley of questions, said that a burglar had just stolen a television set a few blocks away. I didn't even have a pocket or a basket on my bicycle, but I had learned from my father what to say:

"I haven't stole nuthin,' officer," I said, looking my interlocutor in the eye.

I knew what I was saying was true, but still I felt guilty.

The guilt I felt on that street in shorts was the same guilt I felt in long pants, in the student center waiting for someone to validate my presence. Guilt is a feeling necessary for the survival of African-Americans. You have to think about yourself the way the police think about you. You have to have an excuse, a reason to be where you are at all times. You see yourself and other Black people the way the police and the courts and the schools and the banks see you. You are guilty in their eyes until you prove otherwise.[3]

For the police, my straying north of Olympic was how I fell out of one context and into another. And for me, sitting quietly in the entranceway of the student center, I was trespassing until I could prove to the powers-that-be that I was not.

---

[3] You will never prove yourself innocent; just not guilty *this time*.

4.

FINALLY HARRY ARRIVED. He was surrounded by well-wishers whose lives he'd been affecting for decades. He signed programs and shared smiles. He put an arm around my shoulders and pulled me along into the inner sanctum. Harry, who is his own context, saved me from my perpetual fear of being exposed and expelled.

We went to the green room where Hugh and a few others waited. Hugh was, I kid you not, practicing his trumpet. It was only a few notes, but the tone and the man were unmistakable. For a moment I was brought back to a much earlier time in my life, a time when the love of music was a political act as well as an indescribable joy. I was in the sixties and in my teens, and the world was moving toward a form of justice that I could imagine but that I may never reach.

Hugh talked about writing a book, a mystery. Harry was planning a celebration of the Diasporic Black Arts from around the world to be held in South Africa. Quincy (who arrived a few minutes later), I knew, was working on a film about Miles Davis. None of us, it seemed, were working solely on the things that we were known for. Context breakers all, we were moving outward toward other disciplines and ways of expression.

Those few moments in the green room had a lot to teach me, but I didn't know it until I wrote these words (almost as filler) to begin this section of my explorations.

Too soon, we were in the big room where the dialogue was to occur. The house was full. The seats had posteriors in them; the faces were expectant. I started off the event with the words I shared above. I made a joke or two, which is my wont, and the talk began in earnest.

Hugh said things that I had not considered before that night. He called contemporary South Africa the hope of the entire sub-Saharan continent. Here you have a democratic, primarily Black, African nation that has a strong trade history and the potential, at least, for great wealth; a nation whose current history and character is defined by a struggle for freedom; a nation that attained that freedom without resorting to warfare; a nation that is thousands of miles from the United States—which has seen itself as the arbiter of world freedom for more years than, some say, it has a right to.

Mr. Masekela spoke in concrete terms about building a new world. And for the first time I saw a structure of hope that might do for worldwide justice what America has done for (or to) the worldwide economy. Hugh was saying that the future of the world might not be lodged in her most powerful nations but instead in that country which has striven most fervently for freedom against a system which had all of the qualities of modern-day oppressors, apartheid in South Africa being a microcosm of the domination of the Western world (plus one or two) over the so-called Third World.

Suddenly I was elated by the notion that I don't have to look to the conservative thought flooding my country as the only hope (or its opposite) for human liberation on a global scale. Maybe South Africa and other fledgling nations will sway the direction of our world toward a better future. Maybe there are others who can see past the capitalist rhetoric dressed in egalitarian clothing that typifies the pomposity of American political dialogue.

Maybe South Africa is the hope of the world. And if not that nation, maybe it is Venezuela or Vietnam or some other country that has dealt with the imperialism of the twentieth century—and won.

Sitting in that front row, listening to the trumpeter bring me out of an intellectual shadow that (I now see) has darkened all of my years, I began once again to think about context. Being an Ameri-centric nationalist (as we almost all are), I have always thought that it is the African-American experience that is the right and proper gateway to worldwide liberation. The civil rights movement of mid-century America, coupled with the antiwar movement, seemed to ignite a fuse that promised to explode the hegemony of the troglodyte masters of reactionary America—potentially transforming the entire world as it did so.

But that fuse fizzled, and the inexorable domination of the wealthy became ever more powerful. It became apparent sometime in the eighties that we would never displace the rich and reactionary foremen of our democracy's infrastructure with our songs and righteous complaints. Our shadow leaders, like some kind of evil wizards of Oz, give out grants and Grammys, Oscars and lines of tenure, and magically our revolutionary thinkers became grousing members of the establishment.

We can't even free ourselves. At any given moment there are a million people of color in American prisons. Add to that the millions that have been temporarily rclcased only to find themselves back within the system in a few years' time, and you have a method of oppression that goes along unchecked and, even worse, unexamined.

You have liberal African-American politicians that barely pay lip-service to global issues while demanding loyalty to the Democratic Party, a party that couldn't exist without our blind votes but which has rarely made us its primary concern.

We sing a song of freedom while dancing to a tune played by the descendants of our slave ancestors' own-ers. The wealth accrued by the slave masters, having been passed down through their bloodlines, still runs roughshod over our lives. Our liberation never put us in charge of our fate; but this is not our only difference from South Africa and other modern nations. The context of our struggle has an ancient cast to it. We began our fight for freedom when America was the only power we had to contend with. Our enslavement and humiliation were not due to globalization or other international machina-tions.[5] America was our enemy, and therefore America was all we thought about.

---

[5] This claim might not be completely true. The slave trade was, of course, the commerce between nations and the economy that rose from the labor of slaves was certainly international. But we did not experience the global aspects of our oppression. Slavery and the problems that came after seemed to the average American a national problem.

Today little has changed in our community. We still believe that our problems arise from our struggle with white America. We are still, in our minds, separated from the wide world by thousands of miles of ocean that seemingly renders any meaningful relationship with the world at large inconsequential.

We do not know our neighbors in this modern world, and we are therefore living and acting in the past. The America we see and strive against is like the light of a long-dead star. That day is done and a new one has begun. I believe Hugh Masekela was telling me that it is important to see and deal with the world that I'm living in and not the hobgoblins of the past.

Hugh also said that political and economic failure in Africa had to be seen, at least in part, as a South African failure. It was up to the African to resist post-colonialist pressure and to build an Africa worthy of that continent's imagination.

Why is South Africa so important to the politics of liberation? Because it is connected in a real sense to its neighbors both near and far; because it has struggled against the modern foe of imperialist domination and won; because the majority of that nation are members of the once-oppressed class; because they live in the modern world while we here in America are out of touch with the exigencies and logic of global change.

I sat there in the audience listening to Mr. Masekela and hearing what he had to say.

I wasn't the only one.

You would think that that would have been enough. Right then and there, a revolution should have been ignited. Hugh Masekela told me that it wasn't America that was the center of our world system, but (maybe) South Africa instead. Like a modern-day Copernicus, he stood my medieval world view on its head. This was more than enough information for me to go on. But that was only the beginning. Harry Belafonte was yet to have his effect on my ragged and wrong-headed apprehension of the world.

5.

HARRY BEGAN TALKING about the Olympics and African-Americans and the movement for human liberation around the world. He deprecated the need for competition while lauding the physical perfection that so many professional sportspeople attain. He talked about a particular Olympic relay race that was manned by four African-Americans who had all (or nearly all) already won gold medals. No one wondered whether or not the Americans would win, but by how much they would break the world record in doing so. The race began, as Harry told us, and the first length went very well. But when the baton was passed off there was a momentary stutter, just a half of a stumble really, and the race was lost.

Harry told us that he was deeply affected by this slip because for him it stood as a metaphor for the failure of the civil rights movement as it moved past its original phase and into the latter part of the century.

I must say that I found this comparison eloquent and depressing. Somehow the older generation and the younger one had gotten out of synch. The message had been mishandled and the struggle had been derailed. Just a moment's hesitation and we lost the upper hand.

Or, I thought after having listened to Mr. Masekela, maybe we never had it.

Maybe our labors have yet to begin. Maybe everything that we've done so far has been but a prelude to the struggle that's coming. Maybe our suffering over the centuries has yet to be assuaged and rectified. Maybe the millions of dead in Rwanda, Congo, Uganda, and Sudan (not to mention Cambodia and Vietnam) are speaking to us through the ether of our history. Maybe our pain, along with our nation, is not the center of the universe. Maybe our context is deeper and different from the history of those slaves brought to America so long ago to suffer and die. Maybe our race to freedom needs to change direction and cannot be realized in the organized competitions of the West.

If any of these maybes are true, it would mean a monumental change in the attitudes of the descendants of ex-slaves of America. We would have to let go of much of our identity, an identity which is anchored in the victimology that our nation has studied from the first moment Europeans landed on these shores. We might have to see ourselves outside of the context of our ex-slavehood and civil rights in a world where murder has taken the place of diplomacy. We might have to see that we have been occupying the role of oppressor instead of the oppressed. We might have to change our way of thinking if we are to grasp our role (our context) in the modern world.

This is a very disturbing notion. Before now it's all been simple and straightforward: The borders of our known history are the forces of oppression, our ancestors are clothed by us in the sacred garments of victims, and therefore it is easy to see that our responsibilities are nil in the modern world. *They oppressed us*, we say loudly—and rightly, as far as it goes. But as we emerge from history and the world around us transforms, so do we change. We become members of the society, no matter how much that society might vilify us. And our membership carries with it responsibility, not only for our own suffering but also for those that suffer because of us and in spite of our victories.

How can we call ourselves victorious in a real sense when people live in virtual economic slavery in so many parts of the globe?

As long as we see ourselves in the context in which we have been placed by our slave masters (and their descendants and heirs), we will never see the whole world as it has come into being; and as long as this is the situation, we will never be able to know who we are. The glass ceiling imposed by white America is only our first barrier. Civil rights are not informed by Alabama and New York alone. There are people dying and being tortured because of the exigencies of the corporations that we supply with our dollars and by the government we support by being good Democrats and by the cars we drive fueled by foreign oil and the clothes we wear that were made by slaves to our dollars. We are becoming what we have fought so bravely against, and in becoming our enemy, we stumble and fall.

LIKE HUGH MASEKELA, Harry Belafonte spoke of our responsibilities rather than what we are owed. He saw African-Americans as liberators throughout the generations—both past and present. And true liberators don't just free their friends, they make it so that everyone is free.

Sitting there, I thought that it was proper for musicians to take the role of leadership in espousing these egalitarian aspirations. After all, music is the freest of the arts. Paintings and books, ceramics and jewelry, architecture and sculptures are all, ultimately, property. These objects of art, though beautiful and meaningful, often end up in the hands of the wealthy and their bourgeois acolytes. But music belongs to the proletariat, to the sleeping child in her mother's arms, to the poor patrons of local cafés, and to the dispossessed. Music, in its final form, has no body that can be enslaved and sold; it changes with every rendition, it is elusive and universal—not unlike the liberation we spoke about that night.

THE EXHILARATING RHETORIC of that evening delivered to us the same conundrum that I had begun to consider the night I went with my friend to hear the Public Intellectual. He had, I believed, a context in which he saw himself and his art. And though I rejected that synthetic construct for my own work (actually, it was my work that rejected it), I was once again forced to consider it, because without a context you can't have a viable movement, either for yourself or your group.

I was sitting in a room with at least six hundred people listening to a brilliant and accessible rendition of the world we live in and the problems we face. There was no question that the information we received was enough to move on. The older generation could reach out to the young people we had failed to pass the baton off to. We could concentrate on Africa and support those nations that worked for a unified continent. We could make a personal stand against the war that America had declared without any valid reason. We could rally for the poor, the victims of sexism, children riddled with HIV, the imprisoned people of color.

There were a dozen or more actions presented that one might take.

And this, of course, is the same problem that Dr. Diawara exposed in *Conakry Kas*. There is no one unifying battle cry. For South Africa, it had been End Apartheid. For the sixties, it had been End the War. To topple Richard Nixon, it was He's Got the Tapes. One overarching imperative that can be expressed in just a few words makes social action possible.

Often it's just one word. For a dispossessed people that word is *home*. For the slave it is *freedom*. For the capitalist it is *profit*. And for the child, the lonely, and the lost it is *love*.

THERE WAS A dinner after the event. It was also, as with the Diawara dinner, filled with international personages and loud laughing. I didn't stay long, because I was thinking about the problem posed by the speakers.

I left the student center trying to muster a few words that might galvanize the dozen themes I was presented with that night. For me, the word was *context*, but I have an abstract nature. Context is the question, not the answer. What is the context? What is the threat? The crime? What does freedom mean to us? And who are we?

These are the questions that kept me awake yet another night.

6.

THE NIGHT WAS spent in the futile attempt to imagine an answer to a question that wasn't really asked. What is the context that would hold a political movement designed to oppose the forces that represent the Wealthy Dominion that is held over our world today?

There's no question that one of the major problems in today's world is the manner in which the forces of the rich are deployed against the poor. It's a matter of everyday conversation. If a poor man or woman is accused of a crime, most people will tell you that they will receive a different brand of justice than someone who is wealthy. A rich man is much more likely to be found not guilty than a poor son. This is a matter of record. And even if the rich man is convicted, his experience of justice will be different than that of his impoverished counterpart.

I make these claims with little doubt that almost everyone in America (despite their political affiliations) will agree with me. Freedom and equality are, contradictorily, commodities; almost all of us believe that. Maybe, as a rule, justice can't be bought outright, but it sure can be influenced by wealth and what wealth can buy.

True equality for the poor, I thought. Maybe this could be a verbal context. But as I considered the phrase, I realized that there was nothing in it that would tickle the American[6] fancy. Truth is a painful thing to any populace as emotionally deadened and guilt-ridden as are we. Equality is nice but, as I said above, it is a commodity and it's easier to get money than to change the structure of our world. And no one wants to identify themselves with the poor. Poverty is a sin in the religion of Capitalism, and we here in America are the greatest devotees of that Faith.

I went over a dozen or more contextual phrasings. None of them were good enough to present here. To come up with a few words that might stimulate a nation is no easy

---

[6] You may note here that I'm not separating African-Americans from other citizens in this nation. That's because we are Americans. We speak the language, eat the fast food, watch the TV, attend the schools. We've had two secretaries of state in four years' time and we wear the uniform, aim the weapons, and drive the heavy machinery of war. Black America is America.

task. Ad men do it so well. But selling product is different than promoting justice and equality.

Then I realized that I was putting the cart before the horse. I was trying to come up with the catchphrase of my homemade revolution before I was articulate enough with the issues. This is an easy mistake to make. If you identify with the victims of injustice, you think that you know what's wrong. This might be true, on one level—maybe more. But there could be other attendant issues that you have not thought about. For instance, I might see a racial problem in one situation; but if I were to look deeper, I would see that the issues have much more to do with class than with attitudes toward gender or race.

Maybe I should be looking at the threats facing Americans at large and Black America in particular before trying to crystallize that notion into a rallying call, slogan, or motto.

This was my most daunting effort on that sleepless night. It's not that I didn't have material to consider. There were the polluted oceans, the ozone layer, the hundred thousand-plus Iraqi dead, the population of color in prison, HIV among Black teenage girls in the Southeast, the thousands dead every day from disease in Africa, the Patriot Act, the exportation of American labor to the south and east, children shot dead by police in the inner city, children killing other children because they can get their hands on guns so easily, child soldiers in Africa, the lack of a cohesive medical plan for America's poor and working poor, the fact that alcohol consumption is legal but marijuana is not, rampant obesity, rampant consumerism, the fact that most Americans will have to give up on the notion of retirement because they are simply living too long, the fact that our children are undereducated at best and uneducated at worst, drug addiction, alcohol addiction, intolerance, the threat of terrorism, etc., etc.

I had pages of topics that people would agree were major issues, for the contemporary world at large and for America specifically. But I ran up against the same problems I faced before: There are too many issues and no one of them, it seemed, was compelling enough to move a nation.

This alone is a sad state of affairs. The fact of a hundred thousand dead Iraqis in little more than a year should make people feel something. But there are millions dead in Africa and the (self-named) African-American population of the U.S. has yet to make a united stand in protest.

One would think that the Republican Party would balk at the Patriot Act. Aren't they the ones who want less government, states' rights, and the freedom to bear arms?

Spiritually, America resides in Purgatory. We have been anesthetized by disinfected news reports listing the dead in the same way that warehousemen report on inventory. We believe we have knowledge and are unmoved when confronted with atrocities, numbers of dead, obvious inequities, and crimes. We've heard and read it all before on the news. No, we didn't actually see the dead, ripped-up bodies of dozens of children, but we know about them. No, we didn't smell the rotting corpses of entire villages that succumbed to AIDS, exterminations, and strategically engineered famines, but we read about it in the paper. No, we never lived in towns that were bombed until not one building was left standing and no one who survived had all their relatives living—but this, we know, is simply a consequence of war.

This is not to say that Americans won't take action sometimes. For instance, our nation, the whole world, responded with a great outpouring to the victims of the recent tsunami. Tens of millions of dollars were produced instantaneously, almost. Everyone, it seemed, wanted to help. This is a good thing, a wonderfully human response. But when we look closely at it, we can see that it is a very special set of circumstances.

Being a natural disaster, unlike the man-made political and ecological terrors, there is no one to blame or to defend themselves or their actions. The response to the disaster is short-term and not the legal responsibility of major corporations or even governments. The problem is clear, there are no villains to be prosecuted, and once the help is done you don't have to think about it any more.

The troubles in Sudan and Congo are much more complex. You can't just throw down a check and walk away. You've got to study it, think about it, make a moral stand. This *making a moral stand* is where we stutter and fall.

It's midnight. I feel as if I've just come awake from a dream in which I realized something that my waking mind refused to understand. That is: The modern mind in America has come to accept verbal expressions of atrocities as an everyday fact of life; therefore, you cannot simply present, in words, an immense crime and expect the people who hear you to take action.

This is an important idea because if it is true, it indicates that we may have gone beyond the possibility of encapsulating a political movement in a statement or phrase. If we are numbed to ideas represented in words, our hope of changing the world has to transcend linguistic arguments.

This is a very sad state of affairs, but not totally hopeless. It is the problem-formulation moment at the beginning of an experiment. The problem is stated thusly: How do we get the world to see its political and social disasters (i.e. Sudan, Haiti, and Congo) in the same way that it perceived the natural disaster of the tsunami? *And* how do we express the depths of these issues without relying on the simple linguistic devices that worked in the past?

7.

ONE PART OF the answer seems to be to get people to empathize with the victims without the need for recrimination or revenge. We also need to have a trustworthy organization that will make the moral stand in proxy for those moved to want to help.

All right. It's only 12:45 and I have a viable two-step structure that might become the context for political action.

The first thought that came to mind, trying to circumvent the need for catchphrases, was about the large electronic billboards that have been showing up here and there. Like giant television screens, these oversized and animated posters can change images instantneously.

A picture, we're told, is worth a thousand words, and a billboard is worth a million newspapers. And if the placement of that billboard is cunningly considered and the content is controversial enough—one might ignite a nationwide buzz.

So I'm thinking downtown Chicago, Los Angeles, or New York. A skyscraper-sized big-screen TV poster where the content is changed regularly; maybe connected with a Web site to explain the context of the images shown and to give options about how one can take action.

There are many images of the devastation that bedevils people all over the world. Child soldiers, starving populations, rampaging armies . . . the list is endless. If we could present these images on a major scale, we might get enough people to start thinking that something should be done.

Sounds good—but once we have what seems to be a viable notion, we have to question it. And the first question one always has to ask in America is, "How much will this bad boy cost?"

Of course this would be a very expensive undertaking. We're talking millions of dollars. But there's an old saying, "You have to spend money to make money." If you change that saying just a bit, you have "You have to spend money to break money('s stranglehold on your heart)."

The next query is: What makes this different than

newspapers, televisions, and the radio? Isn't all this information already disseminated and ignored?

I'm pretty confident in saying that the regular news outlets will never concentrate on atrocities committed by America (or her allies) or against people whose fates are not considered important to the national interest.[7] There are two reasons why the news media would eschew images that we might find important.

The first is that unless the images and stories pull in viewers or readers, there's a potential problem with advertisers (i.e., income). Especially in television, those ad dollars can make or break a news show in a matter of days. Radio is the same way. And even though the newspapers can support a wider variety of stories and images, I don't believe they would be so political in their approach; and also, the impact of a newspaper wouldn't be the same as a fifteen-story billboard image of the devastation wrought by America.

The second reason to skim over worldwide tragedy is that the corporations that control the media are in bed with other major companies that might well be embarrassed by acts of violence committed in their names.

---

[7] National interest is almost always understood in economic terms. An oil-producing country is the object of national interest. A smaller nation with no vital natural resources that has a madman inducting five-year-old children as combat soldiers and prostitutes is not such an object.

Imagine it. Every day, a different image about suffering around the globe. Children would see it and ask their parents why are those people hurting? We would see it and wonder why we haven't done anything today to ease the pain. And those who make their living off our spending and our labor will think that they need to do something so as not to fall out of favor with their chosen candidate's electorate and stockholders (not necessarily in that order).

To GO ALONG with the billboard, we need a benevolent organization dedicated to world peace and prosperity. The board of directors should be comprised of political, cultural, and religious leaders from every corner of our political spectrum. There should be names recognizable to any American, but there should also be a few international members to open our eyes to the larger world. Our Web site will explain how to make a difference against disease, poverty, and genocide.

Hopefully we will be able to open a dialogue that will force Americans to realize their involvement with political and social instability around the globe. And once we suspect our own culpability, the wound will have been lanced and the draining process will begin.

8.

THAT FLURRY OF thought came at a few minutes after two. For a while then I fell asleep.

9.

THE NEXT THING I knew, the digital face on my cable box was saying 3:33.

I awoke thinking that an electronic billboard was just pie-in-the-sky dreaming. I mean, I don't have the millions of dollars it would take to make that hope into reality. And even if I did, there's nothing to say that it would work. Or maybe, after the first day of exposition, some extremist group (or president) would get our billboard censored for indecency or for inflaming the public.

So I thought that I should consider a different approach in creating a sociopolitical context.

I went back over the ideas for this essay, looking for hints from what I've thought so far.

I kept coming back to the anger that I've been harboring lately toward the Democratic Party.

The majority of Black Americans have been Democrats for at least the fifty-three years that I've been alive. What have the Democrats done for us in all that time? We have the lowest average income of any large racial group in the nation. We're incarcerated at an alarmingly high rate. We are still segregated and profiled, and have a very low representation at the top echelons of the Democratic Party. We are the stalwarts, the bulwark, the Old Faithful of the Democrats, and yet they have not made our issues a priority in a very long time.

Why should we be second-class members in the most important political activities of our lives? Why shouldn't the party we belong to think that our problems are the most important issues in this land?

I'm not saying that we should become Republicans. The Republicans don't care about us either. But at least they don't pretend to be on our side. And you have to admit that, of late, the Republican administration has put Black faces into high-profile jobs that carry clout on the international playing field. I don't have to like Colin Powell and Condoleezza Rice to appreciate that once a Black person has been put into a position of power, the second time around is much, much easier.

We are a racial minority in a country where racism is a

fact of life; a country that was founded on economic and imperialist racism. Taking this reality into account, and adding it to the fact that our issues are regularly put on a back burner, I believe that it is not out of order to send out a call for the formation of a Black Party.

If we had our own political party that paid attention to issues that reflected our needs in domestic and international concerns, many things would change for us. The first thing is that many more of us would be likely to vote. Imagine the interest that young people would have if they felt that we were organizing based on our own interests; they could work for a candidate who represented their issues, they could run for office themselves.

And, even though the party would be based on the racial identity that has been shoved down our throats since the first days we came here in chains, we wouldn't work only for ourselves. We'd argue about medical care and social security and the good jobs that are disappearing from this nation like fleas off of a dead dog's back.

America's corporations, CEOs, and portfolio managers don't have to worry about the euro and the devaluation of the dollar. They belong to an international club. It doesn't matter where the most recent SUV is being produced; what matters is whether my stockholders and I own a piece of the company that makes and sells those cars.

It takes many companies working in unison to make

secure the wealth of American capitalism. Two of the major-interest corporations that facilitate the needs of our most wealthy citizens are the Republican and Democratic (so-called) political parties. They exonerate their actions with numbers of votes, but the wheels they run on are greased by money, and lots of it.

If we took the vote into our own hands, we wouldn't have to ask the Democrats for their support—we could demand it. George Bush, or whoever takes his place, will send for our representatives to come to his home to discuss his plans. This is because they have not yet figured out how to dispose of the vote in the American political system.

Imagine it. We could actually democratize America by taking power away from the two-party system and handing it over to the people. Other special parties would arise, splintering off from the centrist attendants of the rich, once we show them the way.

What I'm talking about here is the beginning of an *American Evolution*; a movement that will create a series of political interest groups that will transform our two-party system into a kind of *Virtual Parliament*. We could construct smaller political groups based on specific interests. There might be a Gay Party with congressional representatives from West Hollywood, San Francisco, and Manhattan. There could be Black Party congresspersons from 'atts, Harlem, the Motor City, and a dozen other inner city bastions. All we have to do is have a fair representation in the House of Representatives to have an extraordinary impact of the wheels of government.

Farmers, women, the aged, angry young white men, and, for that matter, true Republicans might create their own small parties/interest groups. These groups would not only have direct representation in the House of Representatives, but they would also begin to make deals with those individuals running for senator and president, police chief and mayor.

It's past the time when we, Black Americans, can complain about how we are treated without ourselves trying to take the reins of power. A Black Party would be a bold move. Some might say a radical move—too radical. But a country that incarcerates people of color at an eight-to-one ratio to whites has played the race card way before Johnny Cochran. If we could come together and see a way to put balance back in the American political landscape, then we should do it.

Why?

Because if we do not lead, we shall be led. And if those that have learned to despise, distrust, and diminish us are the leaders, then our path will lead even farther away from our homes. We will wake up like strangers in our own beds. We will, and our children will, be walking in uncomfortable shoes to poor jobs. We will be jeered on every corner, and every mirror we come across will distort our image.

JUST SO THAT it doesn't seem that I'm giving short shrift to this argument, let me try to explain why this kind of "political party" will be different from its interest-corporation counterparts. Firstly, this kind of group will be a political unit more than a party. This unit should be patterned after interest groups that form around specific necessities that face our particular community.

As I've mentioned before, I would like to see many of these *units* evolve; but for the moment, let me address the Black Party.

What we need for this group is a short list of demands that define our political aspirations at any given point. These demands might change over time, but at any given moment we should have no more than eight expectations of the candidates or legislation we vote for.

I am not positioning myself as the leader or even as a central designer of this group, but let me put forward a list of possible demands that our *unit* might embrace.

1. A commitment to revamping the legal system and the penal system to make sure that citizens of color are getting proper treatment and that current

inmates will be given the utmost chance to rehabilitate and re-establish themselves in society.

(This rehabilitation will include suffrage for all ex-convicts who have served their sentences.)

2. An expectation that there be equal distribution of all public wealth and services among the citizens, no matter their income, race, or history.

3. A demand that a true accounting for the impact of slavery be compiled by all government bodies in authority over records that give this information.

4. A universal health-care system.

5. A retirement system that will ensure that elder Americans have the ability to spend their later years in relative comfort and security.

6. A commitment to assemble a general history of our nation in both its glory and its shame.

7.

8.

I left 7 and 8 in our list of demands blank because I think you should fill these out. This is, after all, a communal effort meant to bring our intelligences together.

And if you don't feel that you're an affiliate of the Black Party, write your own demands and see what kind of group you might attract. I believe that any political group concerned with the rights of Americans will have at least half of these demands in common.

ONE LAST COMMENT on the idealistic part of this notion:

All Black people don't have to join right off. If we can put together just ten percent of the voting Black population, we will be wielding a great deal of power. Others will join us if our political strategy works. In time, we might tip the scales against the rich and the ultra-rich. If we do that, we might very well make this a better world.

I know that many of you will say that we don't have the time to allow the U.S. to evolve politically. You, as many Americans, believe that our nation faces urgent problems that will have to be solved by the next election—and, later, the elections after that. My answer to this fear is that that is just what they want you to think. Our so-called political parties want you to believe that only they can save you when, really, they have no such intention. The Democrats, the Republicans—they're in business for themselves in this vast Religion of Capitalism. They will never solve

Americans' problems, not fully. We have to strive against the system, change it, make it reflect our inexpert visions of right and good. As long as you vote Democrat, as long as you vote Republican, you will be ensuring that true democracy has no chance to exist. As long as we believe in the fearmongers' light show, the world will suffer under our misguided convictions.

I WROTE THIS piece and was very happy with it. For a long time, I've wanted to make a public argument about the formation of an African-American political party, or unit. We have to be responsible for ourselves, and in order to do that, we have to bring to light all of the possible paths we might take.

But in saying this, I find myself wending back toward the idea of context and our lack of it.

There's no question that a Black voters' party would be a fine context for us and for people of the Black Diaspora around the world. It would be a forum that would express perceptions from the underbelly of the American experience. That experience, I believe, would find resonance on an international scale and help to bring our maverick nation into concert with certain other countries that would like to get along with us.

The only problem is that the formation of a Black Party is on the far side of the context that we need to get to.

How do we get our people to feel strongly about political unity? What in our experience will bring us together?

It's sometime past four. The sun won't be out for a few
hours. If I sleep on it, maybe a Muse or some Trickster will
come to me and I won't have to figure out anything—just act.

10.

IF THE CIRCUMSTANCES of life don't bring us together and force us to act in concert, then we must create our own circumstances. This seems to be a self-evident truth. Being an artist, not unlike the venerable Public Intellectual whose presentation sent me on this path of investigation, I feel that it is my duty to try to construct a system that will illuminate those important issues we all have in common. Only in this light can we see each other and transcend the tyranny of the pocketbook.

That's the only reason I'm writing this piece: to try and figure out how we get together and work as One. There are a thousand reasons for people of color and their supporters in other racial communities to come together, but a thousand reasons may have just as many groups that form around them, each organization claiming that their commitment is the most important. There are Afro-centrists and urban planners, feminists and gays, NRA members and Democrats, conservatives and rap masters, radicals and socialists; there are artists and philosophers, rich businessmen and the cultural guides that have seen themselves as our leaders since the sixties came and went.

The unjust, unjustified, and barbaric war against Iraq is obviously not enough to shake our moral foundations. Our rock-bottom salaries and nonexistent medical insurance coverage doesn't move us to question why. Four million Black men and women going in and out of the prison system must be guilty because they were, or will be, convicted.

Natural reasons are not motivating us to unite and so it seems we have to create a rallying point.

I make this claim with a great deal of trepidation.

My fear comes from the knowledge that I'm not the first late-twentieth-century would-be do-gooder who has come to the conclusion that our context must be fabricated.

Politicians fabricate all the time. They cull the radical fringe and the special-interest groups for commonality and then profess belief where they have none. They promise a *chicken in every pot* or warn about homosexuals or communists. They babble and stutter in public because they think that the common citizen babbles and stutters.

More to the point, they create enemies and threats that bring us together in fear. They see terrorist collusion and weapons of mass destruction behind every beard. They militarize and kiss bloody wounds. They find zealots that actually believe these things and press them into the public eye.

Our politicians are masters at creating context. We come together under the great umbrella of one of the two major (so-called) political parties and ask, *Who am I?* They respond, *You are the innocent victim of those that hate freedom. You are the unknowing pawn of thieves that defraud our great public works. You are a member of a great democracy whose fate it is to protect the world from its own misguided notions and ancient belief systems.*

And we believe this jive. Why wouldn't we? These are our leaders talking. Our notions of human rights and democracy have been cooked up in their mothers' kitchens. They created the language that we were taught in school. Their friends own all of the major media outlets. It is only through their largess that we might have comfort in our lives.

We want to believe in our political leaders. Let me say that again: We want to believe in our political leaders. This phrase by itself is worth much consideration. At first it seems patently obvious and simple—not a very deep statement at all. But of course it is. Our leaders lied about weapons of mass destruction; they lied about Iraqi collusion with fundamentalist Islamic terrorists. And if you're a conservative reading these words, let me modify it for your benefit: Our leaders were wrong about weapons of mass destruction; they were wrong about Iraqi collusion with fundamentalist Islamic terrorists. In either phrasing, we were given erroneous information by people who we want (in the worst way) to believe in.

They gave us the wrong information and still we listen to them as if they were fully capable of telling the truth.[8]

In our everyday lives, this would never fly. If somebody came up to you and told you that it was the guy across the street who vandalized your car and then went with you to beat and torture that man, only to admit the next day that his information was faulty, you would never trust that person again. But when our leaders do the same thing, we act as if it never happened. We don't ask for an accounting.

How can this be? The answer is simple: We are living a life out of context with our own belief systems, with what we believe to be good and right.

"I am not an assassin, a murderer, a thief, a torturer, a sexual deviant, or a criminal of any kind," most Americans would claim. But all of these acts have been carried out in

---

[8] I hope you realize at this point I am not singling out Mr. Bush and his cabal. The Democrats are the same. They lie and mislead. They ignore the truth along with their right-wing counterparts.

our name in the Middle East. We are all culpable for our nation's actions; all of us. But we don't actually feel guilty because in some way we don't acknowledge the crimes. We don't because we want to believe in our leaders and our nation so strongly that lies magically become truths and we are purified in the nearly alchemical process.

We don't ask for an accounting because we don't want to know.

This is the reason that politicians and political leaders can construct moral contexts for us to invest in without having to be answerable for the consequences of our, or their, actions.

I want to create a context, but not like that. I don't want to lie to people in order to get them to move in concert.

But, you might say, I don't have to worry about that. I'm not acting in the service of Big Money or the Military-Industrial Complex.[9] I'm not a flunky of the government or its attendant interest corporations.

I am an idealistic individual trying his best to make a better world.

It sounds very safe and very good. But those fifty-three years have taught me that no human being or human act is wholly innocent.

---

[9] The Military-Industrial Complex is a term coined by one of America's great conservatives—Dwight D. Eisenhower.

So-called idealistic leaders and thinkers have been leading us toward calamities forever.

The terrorist through history is the prime example. Terrorism is almost always anchored in idealism. You belong to a people that you believe have been mistreated and abused by a powerful group which refuses to accept responsibility. You have tried to appeal to this power's human side, you have tried to go to third parties for justice, you have marched and given speeches, you have seen your fellows martyred and assassinated. You have seen children die for no reason, and finally you have decided that your truth is more important than their power. This is a very powerful decision; one not lightly made, and something to be feared. Because when an idealist comes to the end of his or her patience, anything is possible. Suicide is the idealist's sister, murder his unavoidable rendezvous. A man or woman whose belief in their own truth is unshakable becomes a potential nightmare.

How far are we from that nightmare when we decide to create our own context? Hitler did it with European Jewry. Pol Pot did it with anyone who had soft hands. It's easy to make your audience into victims hungry for revenge, but the power and commitment you unleash may be way beyond the actions you wish to take. Look at what has happened in Iraq. We were told that they were in cahoots with Osama bin Laden, and now there are at least a hundred thousand dead, each one of those dead human beings innocent of any crime against us.

Would you want to be the one who made that claim?

11.

IF CREATING A circumstance to stand in the place of a natural context is potentially too dangerous, maybe we should turn to a charismatic leader to guide us safely through the minefield of fanaticism. I say this because I've been told so many times that the problem in this world is that so-and-so died too young. A couple of years ago, I heard another Public Figure who said that it was because Robert Kennedy died that American liberalism lost its way. What might Martin Luther King, Jr. or Malcolm X have done if assassins' bullets had not cut them down in their primes?

If only we had leaders now like we did back then, so many lament. It's hard for me to write these words without a hint of sarcasm. Nostalgia belongs in the retirement home. Any organization, movement, or people who rely solely (or even greatly) on a charismatic leader for their strength and their motivation are in the most precarious political position possible.

"Cut off the head and the body will fall," their enemies murmur.

This is a way to let those enemies dissolve your context. Just put all your belief in one leader and sooner or later you will be lost.

ONE MIGHT SAY that I should end this section with those words. This may be true, but I think that it opens the door to other considerations. We do need leadership. We have to have people that will make decisions and blaze trails; people who will stand up to warmongers and money-lenders; people who might create context, illuminate the darkness with an electronic billboard; people who could organize our vote.

I could spend a lot of time and space here criticizing our current leaders. But what would be the purpose? These leaders, no matter how much they have lost their ways, are not our enemies. If I follow a man or woman who is leading me astray, then I have to accept my own culpability and blindness.

"Didn't you see the millions dying in Africa while your

leaders argued about the references and jokes in the movie *Barbershop*?" someone in a later year may ask.

And how will we answer? If we don't lie, we might say, "I knew what was happening, but I didn't know how to act. I felt powerless and helpless and so I did nothing."

The truth hurts. We all know that. But if we can see that we need leadership and that we don't have the leadership we need, then we might begin to question why.

I believe that a vacuum in our leadership has been caused by a natural conservatism in the Black Community that echoes the smug confidence of America in general. This conservatism harbors a deep dread of our young.

Harry Belafonte had already made the metaphor about passing off the baton when I stumbled upon this thought. Don't get me wrong—I had already seen for myself how the youth and their beliefs have been quashed in our community—but Harry's relay-race metaphor helped me to see what that nullification meant: that not only were the younger generations lost, but that we were the ones who lost them.

This problem has to be approached by utilizing a two-tiered process. First we (the elders) have to realize how we exclude young people from being able to take leadership roles in our community. When did we drop the baton? Why do we celebrate the blues but denigrate hiphop? Why don't we distinguish between major thinkers among our youth and thugs? What are the young people telling us when they talk about bitches and ho's, motherfuckers and niggahs, bling? These are questions that we shouldn't gloss over. We bear the responsibility for the lost generations of our people. Even if we see their actions as self-defeating and self-hating, we have to take responsibility for having allowed this situation to occur.[10]

On the other hand, why do we get so upset when young men and women of African descent also want to identify with their other racial sides?[11] Are we afraid that they're trying to abandon us? Do we want to hold them back so that they don't have a broader and more sophisticated view of their identities? Don't we know that this is their world and it is our job to support them while they gain a solid footing?

These are only the first few questions we should ask and answer. And as we respond, we should edit out all cynicism and derogatory notions from our voices and words. These young people are our only hope. We have

---

[10] And this problem is not only true in the African-American community. The message of hiphop and rap is part of every element of the youth culture. Whites and Latinos, Asians and Africans share this music. Looked at from this point of view, the avenue of hiphop seems to be bringing people together, giving them a voice.

[11] I'm not talking here about the self-hatred that is so common in our history. I'm not talking about people who exclude their African history. But if you have a Swedish parent or a Japanese parent, why wouldn't you see that as a part of your cultural heritage also?

to liberate them where we can, decriminalize them when necessary, detoxify them if possible—but most important, we have to hear what they're telling us and make way for their leadership.

And to the youth I say, you have to take the reins. You have to realize that many members of the older generation have gotten what they wanted out of the Struggle. They aren't worried about the problems of America's urban youth; at least not enough to once again charge the ramparts and put what they have on the line.

Revolutions (both violent and nonviolent) are manned by the young. Older people have retirement accounts and diseases to support, weak constitutions and a justified fear of imprisonment. We have fallen to the rear of the column. You, the urban youth of America, must lead us.

If you (the youth) do not forgive us for fumbling and then take up the baton, our race will be very far behind in the twenty-first century. And if we lose, the world suffers, because most of America is on the wrong road already.

America has carried the notion of property and power to such an intensely negative degree that we have very little room left for humanity and art in our hearts. We work long hours, eat bad food, close our eyes to the atrocities that are committed in our names, and spend almost everything we make on the drugs that keep us from succumbing to the emptiness of our spiritual lives. We gobble down anti-depressants, sleeping pills, martinis, sitcoms, and pornography in a desperate attempt to keep balance in this soulless limbo.

In a world where poetry is a contest at best and a competition at worst, where the importance of a painting is gauged by the price it can be sold for—we are to be counted among the lost. And so when I say that we need leaders and that those leaders must come from our youth, it is no idle statement. We need our young people because without their dreams to guide us, we will only have cable TV and grain alcohol for succor.

12.

THE REST OF my day passed like the first morning after a bad fever. There was a kind of a relief but also some weakness from the disease or, in my case, lack of sleep. I thought that I'd move away from this kind of thinking because I was going to Los Angeles to talk about books and work on films and visit my mom.

I thought that many of my problems (at least my personal ones) would be solved by this journey. One thing that would be addressed by this trip was my context as a writer. In 2005, the mayor of L.A. decided to declare my most recent novel, *Little Scarlet*, as the annual selection for the One Book, One City program of L.A. That meant that all of Los Angeles would be reading and talking about my book and that I would be celebrated and feted around the town.

At the very least, Los Angeles could be my context.

I liked that idea: a writer being associated with a city. His or her works being the focal point for a wide range of citizens of that town. The rest of the world could be ignorant of that writer, but in one concentrated area, they would be well known and well read.

I once knew a poet in Copenhagen named Niels Barfod. We were walking around the city one weekday morning and he was hailed by almost everyone we passed. "Good morning, Niels," they'd say. "Happy birthday, Niels."

After the twentieth greeting like this, I asked, "Does everybody in Copenhagen know that it's your birthday?"

"Yes," he averred.

"How can that be?" I asked.

"It was in the newspaper this morning."

What a context that was. He belonged to that city and that city belonged to him. That might be the perfect place for a writer: not set up in a pantheon of living (or dead) fellow practitioners, but ensconced within an urban setting and claimed in that way.

I SLEPT ON the long flight and then slept at the hotel when I got there. I was awakened once with a call inviting me to come with the mayor to a town hall–style meeting with members of the community of SouthCentral Los Angeles. After some consideration, I agreed to go.

You see, it wasn't a simple meeting. A few weeks before, a thirteen-year-old boy (Devon Brown) had allegedly stolen a car. In the early hours of the morning, the police got on his tail and he tried to get away. At some point, he backed up and hit the squad car. One policeman opened fire, letting off ten shots and killing the boy. These town hall–style meetings were the mayor's way of getting the pulse of the city and allowing some of the angrier citizens to let off steam.

He wanted me to come because I was born and raised in SouthCentral and I had some presence in L.A. (especially since my most recent book was about the '65 Watts riots).

But first we had the announcement of my book as the selection for One Book, One City. That went fine, but it wasn't until the next day that things began to happen.

The public meeting was held in a fire station in the Black and Spanish-speaking neighborhood. A dozen or so people showed up, along with an equal amount of the press, and a full complement of firemen. The mayor was in attendance. The chief of police showed up after a half hour or so.

Everyone spoke their minds. One Black man thought it was time that we stopped blaming the police for the crimes our children commit. "It's the parents," he said more than once, "that should be held responsible."

A few people there agreed with this point of view.

One elderly white man was outraged that the policeman in question had not been arrested for the crime.

The mayor showed concern and made promises that he might very well have intended to keep.[12]

The police chief (Bratton) explained the processes of figuring out whether or not the policeman would be tried on criminal charges. He also talked about how policies governing the interaction between the police and the community would change. There had already been extensive and exhaustive meetings about these policy issues held behind closed doors.

And then there was another guy, a Black man who seemed to be a grass-roots organizer of some sort. He was very impressive. He told the mayor and the police chief that he and his friends were happy to see that there were meetings being held to change public policy. But, he wondered, why weren't the people in that room invited to the policymaking meetings?

"How can you make a policy about us and not have us sitting at the table to comment and amend?" he asked. Maybe those weren't exactly the words he used, but that was the gist of it.

---

[12] Since then, he was voted out of office and so there's a new mayor, but the problems have not changed.

If there was ever an example of someone complaining (justifiably) about being shunted out of context, it was that man at that meeting.

Here I'd flown to L.A. to be feted and celebrated, and instead I found myself being educated about the thing that had been bothering me for the past while. The men of power in that room had a lesson to learn: the lesson of equality. The context was the boardroom where the policies were to be made. The problem was that the community wasn't there. I felt a moment of deep exhilaration. The truth had been spoken, and even if nobody but I heard it, that was enough, at least for the moment. At least I could write about it and say that that's what we have to strive for: We have to sit at the table, not in the yard like a bunch of slaves who are encouraged to believe in the master's beneficence. His intentions toward us are meaningless. It is only our place at the table that makes a difference.

This is what I had been trying to articulate for the past few days and sleepless nights. Our young people need to sit side by side with their elders, equals among them. We need to guide our leaders and in order to guide them we must sit with them; they must sit with us. We have to demand that city boards and town councils, federal and congressional fact-finding groups and police reviews include members of the communities that they serve.

And here I'm not just saying that Black or Brown people should be sitting there. Those Black and Brown people should be active members in the communities that are being considered; not some law grad from Harvard who lives in Brentwood or on Sutton Place South.

Those of us that have positions in the public eye have to join cultural, political, and business boards so that our community is represented when the white world gets together to construct policies and to give out awards for excellence. Even if we can't get them to nominate and award people from our community, at least we can point out that it's not being done.[13]

One of the most important things we can do for our community is to show up to the table and pull out a chair. You may not have been invited, but that's not a problem. Our place at the table is always a possibility, but if we never go there, we will never be there.

I know many people don't involve themselves in these kinds of situations because of anger and trepidation. They know that everyone else at the policy meeting has been there for a long time and in that time they've made decisions that benefited wealthy people (most of whom have

---

[13] This is important to do, because often these boards are blissfully ignorant about their racist exclusions. They meet together and bring up all the names that they always proffer. The names that don't appear, they've never thought of, at least not in that context.

been white), disparaging poor people and people of color in the process. This makes certain potential members angry.

Then there are those who don't know the protocols and the lingo of these policymakers. They believe that they look stupid trying to engage in the dialogues that everyone else enters so fluidly. They offer suggestions that are ignored or belittled or, even worse, shown to be untenable.

These are real issues but not reason enough for us to avoid decision-making roles. Anger, like all other human emotions, is designed to promote our survival. We have to use that anger, express it judiciously. Let the anger bring you to the table. Let the anger raise your voice to speak, to contend, to make them know that we are here as they are: to represent voices that would otherwise go unheard.

Fear can easily be turned into family humor. For the first few meetings, anything you say at the policy meeting may not make sense. You come home and tell your spouse, "Baby, I really made a fool outta myself today." Then you explain and consider. You talk it out with your friends and loved ones. At the next meeting, you'll find that you are better prepared. By the fifth meeting, you will be holding your own.

They don't invite us to the table and we don't demand our place there. If this situation continues, we will never beat out a place for our social context; our voices will never be heard—by them or by us. We are responsible for Black girls with HIV. We are responsible for genocide in Africa. We are responsible when everyday white people say, "I never knew," about us, our history, and our issues.

It is time for us to pull ourselves into context. That empty chair at the table is why our voices go unheard. It's all good and well to be athletes and singers, actors and novelists. But we are not only performers. We are also the rank and file, the eyes and ears and voices of a people. And even though there may be twenty opinions among any three of us, we are still related and together. And we can make a difference, but first we have to peer up out of the foxhole and see the lay of the land.

13.

EVERYTHING THAT I could think about my life out of context came together in L.A. in that fire station. From the microcosm—me sitting at a table reminding everyone else that I'm there—to the macrocosm—where all citizens who are committed to equality for people of color in America and the world vote as one to extinguish the capitalist dominion over our daily lives.[14] There's a great deal of

---

[14] This is not a communist, or even a deeply socialist, sentiment. What I am saying is that we, Americans of every stripe, must know the difference between capitalism, freedom, and democracy. At its best, the capitalist model is closest to fascism. You have that pyramidal structure with the Great Leader on top and everyone else connected in lessening realms of power. There is no such thing as freedom of speech or equality within corporate structure. That wouldn't work.

I'm not negating this economic system, I'm simply saying that at times it comes into conflict with the spirit of democratic American beliefs and rights.

danger in committing our lives to real revolution. If we try to create context as our corrupt politicians do, we run the risk of becoming even greater criminals. And yet if we turn away, genocide will be committed in our name, paid for with our dollars.

There's no getting away from it: We have a tightrope to walk. The older generation, many of us, have comfortable jobs and cable TV to give us comfort. We don't have to act out of concert with the Wagnerian opera that is America-at-large, an opera that has added blackface to prove a lie. But it is still a lie. People are suffering and dying because of our inability to engage and help change the world. The young people know this, but they don't have access to our hearts. They express this frustration in music and we criticize them for it.

We say, "You are disrespectful and self-hating."

"We are your children," they reply.

The voices are loud, but all ears are filled with the cotton that was harvested long ago when we were still slaves producing for massah.

THE CONTEXT IS US. We must make concessions with our brothers and sisters. We must come up with a basic credo like: "All our lives and dreams are sacred; now, how shall we live together in this one great house?"

●

I ONLY HAVE a few more words to add here. There might be one or two other ways of seeing ourselves and understanding how we can deconstruct our mental prisons. The next couple of sections will address these ways.

14.

ONE TOOL THAT is greatly undervalued in the realm of literature (and therefore the rest of culture) is science fiction. This form of fiction has many different ways of pulling us out of our everyday mindsets and putting us into contemplative modes. For instance, a book of this sort might move your consciousness fifty years into the future or a hundred years back. From that point of view, we can look back (or forward) at ourselves with the imposed objectivity of a removed narrator.

This displaced quasi-objective point of view allows for a dialogue to occur within the mind of the reader. The dialogue is between two voices, both of which belong to the reader. One voice is the imagined innocent in the distant time, while the other is the reader defending our time (the present).

A question is asked from the ether—"How does a person in your era spend their time?"

"They wake up early and go to work," the present-day voice responds.

"Do they enjoy their labors?"

"Sometimes, but not usually. Work has an alienating affect on most people, both in the economic and the emotional senses of the term."

"But they are very advanced technologically," the temporally removed voice says. "How much of their lives are spent at these alienated jobs?"

"If you take away eating, preening, sleeping, commuting, self-medicated states, and social responsibilities," you reply, "then the average worker has about six percent of his or her daily life for personal pursuits. That plus two weeks' vacation, when they most often get sick."

"Why do people allow themselves to suffer such inadequate existences?"

"It's the only way you can survive in the modern world," you reply, but in the back of your mind you wonder why. "Most people only make enough money to pay their bills. If they stopped working they would starve."

"But they have enough disposable income to wage wars and to build giant edifices. They have enough money for wasteful gas-burning automobiles," the removed voice challenges. "They could make clothes and machines that would last a lifetime but they do not. They could all share in the absolute profit of their society, and then there would be enough for all."

"But that's against human nature," you reply. "Humans are naturally lazy and shiftless. If one man could share in another's labor, he would become a malingerer and then nothing would get done."

"Do people in your era really have such a low estimation of human nature?"

"It is a fact," the current-day you replies. "It has always been so."

"But didn't cavemen and early human societies have a kind of partial socialism?"

"They were primitives," you say, and the irony becomes almost apparent to you.

The science fiction story is almost always a criticism of the lives we are living today. Once we can imagine a different world or technology then we see ourselves in a new light. We are able to question the contexts of our lives that have hitherto seemed absolute.

CREATING THIS KIND of fiction is easier than it seems. You don't have be a writer; all you have to do is think about it. Ask a question.

"If everyone had all they needed, how would the world look?"

Then answer it.

There are a million questions and for each one there are myriad answers. Once you begin to think outside of the system that defines you (i.e., gives your life its context, or lack of one), you will be able to articulate the questions that will lead to a deeper understanding of our place in the world.

If we could create, in our minds, a wholly different world and then imagine how we would live in that world—then we could see the flaws in the way we live today. That might not change our lives in the physical sense, but it would at least open our minds enough to be able to accept arguments outside of the ones given by our so-called experts, professional politicians, laws and lawmakers.

If we allowed ourselves to speculate on the two words *what if*, we would be committing an act of rebellion that even the FBI and the CIA, backed up by the Patriot Act, would be powerless to counteract.

15

ONE OTHER THING I have to say about life out of context has to do with something I brought up in my first monograph, *Workin' on the Chain Gang: Shaking off the Dead Hand of History*. In that book, which was primarily a layman's criticism of capitalism, I tried to talk about the different tools we need to develop in order to counter the domination of the powers that be (those powers being fueled by Capital). One subject I broached was the use of truth in everyday life. I contended that each and every one of us should tell the truth at least once a day; that truth being different each and every day and reflective of our real feelings and perceived notions of the world.

I have found, in the years since writing that book, many people have wanted to talk to me about truth and its uses. Most people recognize that we lie and listen to lies for most of our waking hours. We lie about our salaries, our physical prowess, our experience, our education, our amorous conquests. We wear clothes to hide our physiques, and we buy property beyond our means. We brag, reinterpret history, and often lie just for the hell of it.

We are told lies by TV ads, politicians, newspapers, radios, and many of the people we meet. If someone were to ask you how many truths you heard in a day, you would most likely say, "None."

The most flagrant and deleterious lies are when we remain silent. Our silence is what gives strength to our enemies. When we reflect on the cost of Iraq's democratic elections, do we wonder, Was it worth it? When we see old men and women shuffling down the streets, are we aware of the pain they endure? Do we give voice to that pain? When we see homeless men and women sifting through the garbage for food and recyclables, do we believe that our fellow citizens should be reduced to this level?

If we see something wrong, something unjust, and we remain silent, we are perpetuating the lie that we agree with things the way things are. If we see injustice and say nothing, then we are part of the mechanism of that injustice. There is no way that we can belong to society and remain silent.

Silence truly is death.

It's easy enough to ask one to speak up, but the reality of voicing the truth (as you see it) can be very taxing. All you have to do is take a short walk in most neighbor-hoods and you will see mountains of injustice. If you were to speak out at every single infraction of morality, you might never be quiet or have time for the pretty little lies that make life bearable.

How do I come to the truth in my everyday life? This is a major concern, and one worth many days of contem-plation; maybe a whole lifetime of thought. Truth is dif-ferent for each one of us. We all see the world from a unique viewpoint and have learned to interpret phenom-ena in innumerable ways. We are trained to lie and pre-varicate in order to be sociable and antiseptic. Our feelings and opinions should be kept to ourselves, we think. We should defer to our leaders, and their experts, when the world doesn't seem to provide sensible answers.

We know that TVs are filled with untruths, that politi-cians are liars, that most things we are told by neighbors, friends, and acquaintances are either conscious lies or lies that have been spread by word of mouth. People lie to get ahead, to hold others back, to make a profit, or to make themselves seem grander in the reflection of your eyes.

We live in a system of lies and are held in thrall to their misdirections.

Why do we need to break this system down? Because we can never arrive at our doorstep if we are given the wrong directions.

How do we break this system down? By refusing to participate in it.

I don't mean that you have to stop with the pretty little lies we all adore.

"You're looking better," you say to the man with the gray pallor who's just been released from the hospital.

Why not say it?

But when that man recovers and he tells you that the homeless man on the corner is just lazy, it's your duty to say, "No, he's suffering from a mental illness and cannot care for himself. There is no sufficient health care to take him because of our president's tax breaks, and so that man lives in the alley because we have put him there."

The truth shall set you free.

16.

OUR DESIRE FOR freedom and justice needs to be put into a viable context. In order to create this motive structure we have to question ourselves and our deepest beliefs, we have to call upon our children to lead us, we have to work in concert politically and otherwise, we have to tell (and hear) the truth whenever we can, and we have to commit ourselves to a better world beyond personal and nationalist self-interest.

These words are easy to write, but the simplicity ends there.

Probably the greatest difficulty in achieving these grandiose ideals is in choosing the process which we use in attaining them. Most of us are everyday people with spotty educations and lopsided notions of how the world works. In order to achieve a better world, we have to start working at it, and we are afraid that we don't know what to do. This is a valid fear; more than that, there is Truth in the fear: we don't know the right actions to take most of the time. We don't know whom to trust.

This situation is much like children when they're small. They might be afraid of a doorknob and all that brass orb means to them. It opens a door that might be left ajar to dangerous strangers; it opens onto a world that is frightening and new; it locks behind them if they wander out and then they fear that they will be separated from what they need for protection.

We know that they will find their way, that in a week's time we'll be seeing them out the door and down the stairs into the yard. Slowly, day by day, our children learn the ways of the world. Their inquisitiveness and natural intelligence show them the way (along with our guidance).

The child is driven to move outward and to understand the world and their place in that world.

Are we very different?

There is much to learn, but it is not beyond us. All one has to do is decide on one global issue that needs their attention. Isolate that need and learn all you can about it. That issue, that need is like a single strand of string sticking out of a seemingly hopelessly knotted ball of twine. You work at that end of the knot intent, ultimately, on unraveling the whole complicated puzzle. On your way, you will come across other strands related to or tied up with the thread you're working on. At this point, you might start working on the new problem; or you may continue with your original string, all the time remembering that your goal is to disentangle the whole ball.

I know this simile lacks a concrete handle, so let me try to give an example.

Let's say that your primary love is for children, their safety and protection. As you examine the welfare of children around the world, you realize that many thousands, maybe even millions, of children are pressed into being soldiers, prostitutes, labor slaves, and into situations where they are the helpless victims of war, famine, and plague. This becomes your bit of string. You don't have to be an expert or anti-American or absolutely sure of every step to commit yourself to this issue. Children are dying. That's enough for you.

As you join organizations and study the problem, as you donate your time and money to this issue, all you have to do is keep one thought at the back of your mind—that the problems of the world are all connected. The world economy impacts these children. The deaths of parents brought on by plague and war makes them into orphans. Deviant foreigners with aberrant sexual appetites prey upon them. Ignorance among your fellow citizens, friends, and neighbors worsens their plight. The World Bank cannot consider these children above the profit margins they demand.

As you worry the knot at your end of the tangle, others who might heed these words work from other places. One man is concerned about farm workers in the Third World that are marginalized to the point of starvation by agribusiness. A woman in Detroit begins to work for prison reform in order to deal with the problem of our bloated penal systems. Someone else is working to form the Black Party so that the voices of African-Americans will be heard outside of the soundproofed room that has been our election booth.

All of these individuals are working on the same problem. Each one has found a different way into the fray. The only major concern left is that they might not recognize each other as brothers and sisters in the same struggle. They might not realize that in working for one good, we are necessarily working for all good. We must try to remember that we are all only partially informed; that someone working on a different tangle may be helping us along the way. We must remember to use our hearts whenever possible and to believe in the passions of others.

THE MAJOR PROBLEMS left are those people and organizations that further complicate the troubles of the world while saying that they are trying to help. The World Bank, the U.S. armed forces, corporate invaders, and racial haters fall into this category. They are not easy to pin down. All of them say that they're trying to make a better world, and they have well-practiced oratory to prove it.

We have to have a system to test those that claim to be working with us. That system is a series of questions that must be asked of anyone claiming to be working for equality and justice in the world.

First, any action they propose cannot include an aggressive act of war. Violence against non-combatant civilians can never be tolerated. Taking away the authority of a people always has to be a last resort, and the people proposing this takeover can never evince happiness in the act, nor can they profit from it. We should never take over the economy of a nation, nor should we give that nation's economy over to our capitalist representatives.[15] We should never support anyone who claims superiority over other cultures, belief systems, races, or genders. Nationalism that is blind to foreign interests must be avoided. And the intention of every action must have connected with it the notion of human liberation, survival, or empowerment.

This is at best a limited list. It will come up against severe tests along the way. For instance, what do you do when your investigations lead you to believe that the Hutus are planning a mass genocide of the Tutsis? What

---

[15] Indeed, we should try to limit corporate influence in any political arena, either at home or abroad.

do you do when a mad dictator is murdering his people? How do we respond to powerful nations like China when they crush their children and workers? How do you deal with your legitimate brothers and sisters in the Struggle when your works come into conflict with theirs?

I certainly don't have all the answers. I don't even have most of the questions. But I do believe that working toward a concrete context by these means will lead somewhere. I do believe that a lack of context is the problem and that each and every one of us has the power to work toward a solution. I do believe that we need to build a table and sit at it together, including as many people as we can to develop our policies, our agendas, and our goals.

Economic globalism has pressed many lives out of context. It's about time we push back.